MICHAEL ROSEN
and SUSANNA STEELE

Inky
Pinky
Ponky

COLLECTED PLAYGROUND
— RHYMES —
Illustrated by Dan Jones

D1355097

PictureLions
An Imprint of HarperCollinsPublishers

K. STORES

JOHNNY McCANN
NEWSAGENT AND CONFECTIONER

CHE

PRESCRIPTION

P.K. penny a packet
First you lick it
Then you crack it
Then you stick it to your jacket
P.K. penny a packet

What's your name?   Johnny McCane
Where do you live?   Down the lane
What's your shop?   Lollipop
What's your number? Cucumber

Ittle, ottle,

Mrs Mop owns a shop
All she sells is lollipops
Red white and blue

OTHERS FOLLOW

AACS
GATE, LONDON EC

Delightfully R

SARSAPA

Plainsy went to work, Plainsy bought a shirt
Plainsy wore it, Plainsy tore it, Plainsy what a twerp

Seashells, cockleshells
Lillywhite over

I like lemonade cos lemonade goes 'pop'
There's 2p off the bottle, if you take it to the shop

First published in Great Britain by
Granada Publishing Limited in 1982
First published in Picture Lions in 1990
This edition published in 1993

9 8 7 6 5 4 3 2

Picture Lions is an imprint of the Children's Division,
part of HarperCollins Publishers Limited,
77-85 Fulham Palace Road, Hammersmith,
London W6 8JB

Printed in Great Britain by BPCC Paulton Books

Inky pinky ponky, daddy bought a donkey

Inky Pinky Ponky

Donkey died, daddy cried, inky pinky ponky

I went to the pictures tomorrow
And took a front seat at the back
I fell from the pit to the gallery
And broke a front bone in my back
The lady she gave me some chocolate
I ate it and give it her back
I phoned for a taxi and walked it
And that's why I never came back

Oliver Oliver Oliver Twist
I bet you five dollars
You can't do this
Bend your knees
Stand at ease
Quick march
Over the arch
Oliver Oliver Oliver Twist

Skinny Malink melodeon legs
Big banana feet
Went to the pictures
And couldn't find a seat
When he found a seat
He fell fast asleep
Skinny Malink melodeon legs
Big banana feet

Please keep off the grass, sir
To let the ladies pass, sir
You know the rules
You silly old fool
So please keep off the grass, sir

Please keep off the grass, sir
To let the donkeys pass, sir
You know the rules
You silly old fool
So please keep off the grass, sir

Humpty Dumpty sat on a wall
Humpty Dumpty had a great fall
All the king's horses
And all the king's men
Trod on him

Humpty Dumpty sat on a chair
While the barber cut his hair
Cut it long
Cut it short
Cut it with a knife and fork

Are you the guy
That told the guy
That I'm the guy
That gave the guy
The black eye?

No I'm not the guy
That told the guy
That you're the guy
That gave the guy
The black eye

My old man's a dustman
He wears a dustman's hat
He bought two thousand tickets
To watch a football match

Fatty passed to Skinny
And Skinny passed it back
Fatty took a rotten shot
And knocked the goalie flat
Where was the goalie
When the ball was in the net?
Halfway up the goalpost
With his trousers round his neck

Singing:
Umpah umpah
Stick it up your jumper
Rule Britannia, marmalade and jam
We threw sausages
At our old man

They put him on the stretcher
They put him on the bed
They rubbed his belly
With a five pound jelly
But the poor old soul was dead

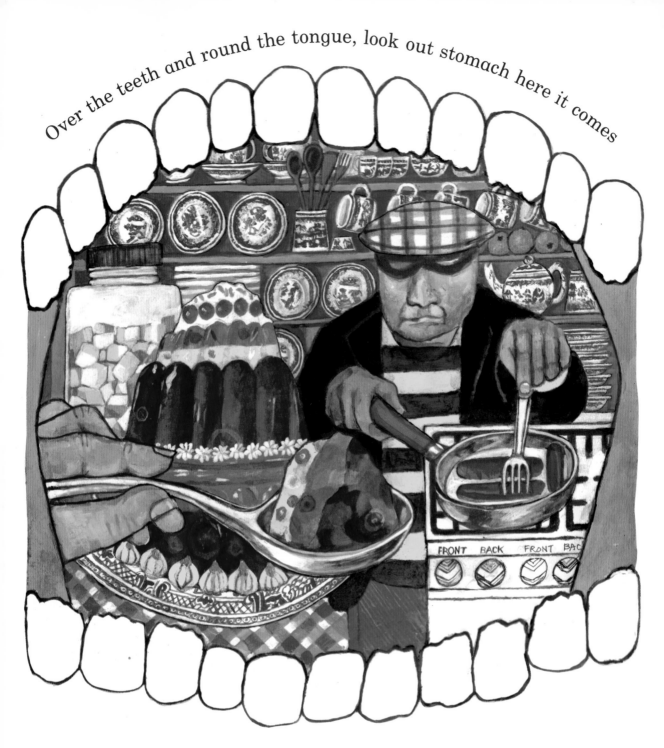

Jelly on the plate   Sausage in the pan   Sweeties in the jar
Jelly on the plate   Sausage in the pan   Sweeties in the jar
Wibble wobble   Sizzle, sizzle   Pick them out
Wibble wobble   Sizzle, sizzle   And eat them up
Jelly on the plate   Sausage in the pan   Sweeties in the jar

Granny's in the kitchen
Doing a bit of stitching
In came a bogeyman
And chased granny out
BOO!

'Well' says granny
'That's not fair'
'Well' says the bogeyman
'I don't care'

Granny Granny Grey can we go out to play?

We won't go near the water to chase the ducks away

Don't go to granny's any more, more, more
There's a great big copper at the door, door, door
He'll grab you by the collar
And charge you half a dollar
So don't go to granny's any more, more, more

I'm a little bumper car, Number 48
Swish round the corner and put on me brakes
Policeman came over and put me in jail
And all I drank was a small ginger ale

Good Queen Annabella
Washed her hair in sarsaparilla
Sarsaparilla turned it yellow
Good Queen Annabella

Good Queen Christine
Washed her hair in Vaseline
Vaseline, turned it green
Good Queen Christine

Queenie Queenie Caroline
Washed her hair in turpentine
Turpentine made it shine
Queenie Queenie Caroline

Tell tale tit
Your tongue shall split
And all the donkeys in the land
Shall have a little bit

Wee Willy Winky went to town

with his knickers hanging down

As I went up in my penny balloon
My penny balloon went pop
I fell right down to the deep blue sea
And I caught a fish in my frock

She stood on the bridge at midnight
Her lips were all a quiver
She gave a cough
Her leg fell off
And floated down the river

The GARDEN OF EDEN

Adam and Eve
In the Garden of Eden
Admiring the Beauties of Nature,
The Devil jumped out
Of a Brussels sprout
And hit 'em in the eye with a potato

Ladles and Jellyspoons
I come before you
To stand behind you
And tell you something
I know nothing about
Next Thursday
Which is Good Friday
There'll be a Mothers'
Meeting
For Fathers only

Wear your best clothes if you
haven't any
And if you can come
Please stay at home
Admission free
Pay at the door
Take a seat
And sit on the floor
It makes no difference where you sit
The man in the gallery is sure to spit

I had a little brother
His name was Tiny Tim
I put him in the bath-tub
To teach him how to swim

He drank up all the water
He ate up all the soap
He was ill in bed last night
With a bubble in his throat

In came the doctor
In came the nurse
In came the lady
With the alligator purse

He's sick, said the doctor
He's sick, said the nurse
He's sick, said the lady
With the alligator purse

Out went the doctor
Out went the nurse
Out went the lady
With the alligator purse

I know a teddy bear
Blue eyes, curly hair
Roly, poly down the street
Knocking people off their feet

Our teacher is no good
Chop him up for firewood
If he is no good for that
Feed him to the pussy cat

If your teacher interferes
Tie him up and box his ears
If that does not serve him right
Blow him up with dynamite

Glory glory hallelujah
Teacher hit me with a ruler
The ruler snapped in half
All the kids began to laugh
And they all went
Marching on

No more Latin
No more French
No more sitting
On the old school bench

School dinners
School dinners
Iron beans
Iron beans
Sloppy semolina
Sloppy semolina
I feel sick
I feel sick
Get a bowl
Quick

On top of a mountain
All covered in sand
I hit my poor teacher
With a great elastic band

Please Miss, me mother Miss
I've got to tell you this Miss
That I, Miss, won't Miss
Be in school tomorrow, Miss

Our teacher is a funny one
Got a nose like a pickled onion
And a face like a squashed tomato
And feet like flat fish

We break up
We break down
We don't care
If the school falls down

Here are some more Picture Lions

for you to enjoy